MOMENTS IN TIME

UPLIFTING POEMS FOR GRIEVING HEARTS

HILARY STEEL

CONTENTS

To Harry and Jennifer Steel

INTRODUCTION

I spent over eight years of my life caring for my parents at home until they died three months apart. Mum first and then dad, who I honestly believe, died of a broken heart. I have always used the written word to express my private emotions, from journaling those teenage years to writing funny ditties to perform in front of family and friends. Poetry then became a comfort blanket, a method to come to terms with my grief.

A chance conversation with Alex, owner of William Whitmey Funeral Directors in Sittingbourne, Kent, allowed me to begin a role I was curious about. After delivering the eulogy at my mum's funeral, I knew I wanted to look into becoming a Funeral Celebrant further. My dad knew about this decision and we spoke about the first family Alex gave me to look after. He was proud of me. I delivered this funeral just four days after he died. Working with Alex has become an important part of my life and although I am an Independent Celebrant, I am proud to be part of 'Team Whitmey'.

Since then, I have written over three hundred poems for grieving families. Many of these are personal to each family, but the collection in this book will hopefully bring comfort to anyone experiencing their own grief journey. I believe that grief is a process, and it certainly isn't linear. Sometimes you simply have to let it play out and accept that it will never completely disappear.

This book is a safe space for grieving hearts and minds to wander and remember the ones they love capturing their own *'Moments in Time'.*

AUTHOR'S NOTE

I wrote these poems in specific moments in time, and they appear in their near raw form. As well as finding comfort in these pages, I invite you to use these poems in any way you wish. All I ask is that you credit me should they be recited in public.

I truly understand how chaotic grief is, but the best piece of advice I received was...'It's okay to smile and laugh in memory of a person you love.'

ONE

—— ◆ ——

MOMENTS IN TIME

When the words you speak cannot express
Exactly what you feel,
It's time to look back in the past,
To focus on what was real.

Was there a moment when
You walked upon the shore?
Talking about future plans,
That now exist no more?

Close your eyes and remember,
How that made you feel,
And know that deep inside,
This can still be real.

Moments in time,
Are simply the key
That needs to be turned,
To bring you back to me.

Memories are precious,

And long shall they remain.

Deep within my heart,

Until we meet again.

Two

I Struggle Too

My personal experience with grief has taught me a lot. I find it comforting to write poetry when these moments creep up on me. This poem is one of those *moments*.

I'm that girl, standing behind in the queue,

The one with her eyes fixed firmly on her shoe.

I'm that girl wearing shades in the dark,

The one whose eyes have lost their spark.

Those same eyes sting from all the tears shed,

As I battle emotions fighting in my head.

One day I'm okay, with happy memories to share,

The next I'm in a nightmare, where I don't care.

I feel abandoned, but people think I'm strong,

Portraying strength doesn't make you belong.

We proudly wear masks that convincingly hide,

The truth of the pain we feel inside.

How much brighter could the world look

If starting a conversation was simply all it took,

To speak of a world that doesn't look so bleak

Giving us the chance honestly to speak.

A friend, a stranger, someone who stands near,

Offering unconditionally a listening ear

To someone like me who struggles too...

We're not so different, me and you.

THREE

— ◆ —

I HEAR YOUR NAME

I hear your name on the whispering wind
Where our dreams are still alive.
Your legacy rests with the children you bore,
What you lovingly taught will allow them to thrive.

I hear your name as the gentle rain falls,
Droplets landing on the ground.
Mesmerising shapes
To you this moment is bound.

I hear your name as the sea reaches the shore,
Remembering our walks along a sandy beach.
If I close my eyes and breathe in the sea air,
I feel you're almost within reach.

I hear your name in my dreams at night,
You're there when I fall asleep.
Our closeness was always our magical bond,
And this feeling, I will always keep.

Four

―― ◆ ――

Grief's Heartbeat

There's a heartbeat hidden behind the grief,
Stolen emotions by a capable thief.
Grief and love so powerfully entwined,
Playing tricks upon the grieving mind.

This new journey is one you must ride,
You can't escape, there's nowhere to hide.
To have loved deeply is the cause of this pain,
Knowing, that your love wasn't in vain.

Those priceless memories still live on,
Something triggered like the words of our song.
These feelings of sadness serve to teach,
A less painful future is within our reach.

You learn how powerful chosen thoughts may be,
Clearing the fog, allowing you to see
The truth of what your broken heart is feeling,
It's a painful process, but it's known as healing.

FIVE

— ◆ —

A Chosen Moment

Life is challenging but we all have a choice
To explore options and use our own voice.
The chosen path may not always be clear,
Taking you away from all you hold dear.
Perhaps time is against you, fleeing past?
A long-forgotten memory surfacing at last.

Life offers chances, there to embrace,
Opening the door to a harmonious place.
A chosen decision may not always be right,
But some things in life are worth the fight.
Watch as the clouds form patterns in the sky,
Understanding that it's never truly goodbye.

Life shows us that there is hope,
You'll be strong and manage to cope.
A chosen action may lead us astray,
Understanding you were powerless to stay.
Together we battle storms our heads held high,

Feeling close to you, looking up in the sky.

Life adapts to the changing seasons,

It is not for us to questions those reasons.

A chosen feeling allowing us to connect,

With a lifetime of memories and to reflect.

Breathe in deeply, allow yourself to believe,

It's okay to miss you, it's okay to grieve.

Six

Love Lives On

Sometimes I'm scared to spend time alone,

Never quite sure where my thoughts will roam.

I let them flow

Helpless to show

Grief at losing everything I've known.

My thoughts are chaotic, sometimes unstable,

I can't fight it, I am unable.

Let them run

Do not shun

Raw emotion for which there's no label.

Fresh air is a friend, but also a foe,

As up in the clouds, there's nowhere to go.

Don't fight the pain

It's nature's rain

Nurture yourself and peace will grow.

Grief creeps up without a sign,

No schedule it eats time,

Let it run free

Soon you'll see

Balance will again align.

SEVEN

—— ◇ ——

IT'S LONELY HERE WITHOUT YOU

It's lonely here without you,

But I knew you couldn't stay.

The look of peace in your eyes

Gives me comfort every day.

People whisper about the circle of life,

I've witnessed this in truth.

The freedom to choose the path,

Now rests within the hands of youth.

The lessons you have taught me,

I will always hold so dear.

And in those dark sad moments,

I know that you'll be near.

Family is not bound

By just the ties of blood.

And from your sad passing,

I'll search for something good.

It's lonely here without you,

But I knew you couldn't stay.

I'll always treasure our memories,

They'll never go away.

Eight

A Part of Me

Let's walk and remember together,

A bond of love that lasts forever.

Your heart continues to beat with my own,

As I bring all your loving memories home.

Let sadness fade and a smile shine through,

Happy moments where I think of you.

Time plays tricks on a grieving heart,

As a life without you I now must start.

Let's walk and feel the sand in our toes,

What will happen after sunset, nobody knows.

But I feel safe knowing that you'll always be,

A part of my heartbeat, a part of me.

NINE

— • —

AS THE DOOR OPENS

It's loud out there, let's shut it out,

Scupper those worries, dilute that doubt.

As the door opens, it's time to leap

These are your memories, to treasure and keep

In your heart, where they will remain cherished,

None of them tainted, none of them blemished.

There's a silence in the air, that can deafen the soul,

Embrace the quiet as grief takes its toll.

As the door opens, it's time to run,

While feeling pride in how far you've come.

Understand that memories are yours to keep,

In every waking moment and as you sleep.

The honesty of love flows without pausing for breath,

Showing you reasons not to fear death.

As the door opens, don't be afraid to cry,

Live in the moment, don't question why.

Step into a future where pain can be spared,

Knowing deep down how much they cared.

TEN

— • —

DAD YOU WERE THE FIRST MAN

Dad, you were the first man who showed me

How to build my life.

Now I'm in the arms of a man I love,

About to become his wife.

I wish that you were here

To walk me down the aisle,

But as the tears wash over me,

I'll just imagine your loving smile.

Dad, you were the first man who showed me,

How to make my dreams come true.

As I stand here in my wedding gown,

I'm thinking only of you.

Although the urge to cry

Plays heavy on my mind.

I will always remember you, dad,

For being funny, caring and kind.

Dad, you were the first man who showed me

That love bears no conditions,

And if I want to achieve a goal,

How to chase my own ambitions.

I've listened to all the lessons,

Where you showed me I can.

Dad, I'll always respect you,

And you'll always be the first man.

Eleven

— ◦ —

I Remember

I remember as a child sitting on your knee,

Laughing at those stories you made up for me.

I remember walking with you hand in hand,

Grinning at the shapes, we dug out in the sand.

I remember smiling, resting in your arms.

Enchanted by the tales you told full of magical charms.

You see, there are some memories that will never fade,

That are kept alive and very often replayed.

The grief I have is painful, but deep inside I smile,

Knowing I got to hold your hand, if only for a while.

In my memories, I smile and continue to believe

In the love you showed me although it hurts to grieve.

I remember getting married, you walked me down the aisle,

Both of us too petrified to even crack a smile.

I remember how you fixed things, even those not broke,

How I'd burst out laughing every time you told a joke.

You made a point to teach me, that people come and go,

And accepting things change will allow me to grow.

You've been right about so many things, and that I thank you for,

I will always remember you as the first man I adore.

Twelve

— • —

I Thought of You Today

I thought of you today and at first I felt quite sad,

Then I had to smile, I'm lucky you're my dad.

A child grows up wrapped in fatherly love,

Now when I think of you, I simply look above.

I thought of you today and closed my eyes to see,

Memories of me as a child sitting on your knee.

Your arms wrapped around me, softening my cries,

Happiness for my future beaming in your eyes.

I thought of you today and how much you cared,

And how you were the light at night when I was scared.

Your powerful protection fills me with such pride,

I know deep down within me, you're still by my side.

I thought of you today as people gathered round,

And in your loving memories I will myself surround

Conversations may well be over, but I am not afraid,

I understand dear dad, there's no way you could have stayed.

I thought of you today, sitting with my mum,

Laughing together at all the things you've done.

I'm lucky to have you as my loving dad.

I thought of you today, and now I feel less sad.

THIRTEEN

DON'T LOOK BEHIND

Don't look behind, there's nothing there to see.

Look right in front of you as that's where I'll be.

I'm waiting, ready to hold your hand,

By your side you'll feel me as I proudly stand.

I'll always watch over you from not too far away,

Guide your dreams at night and push your dreams by day.

If you want to feel me smile then do not cry,

Breathe in deeply and look up to the sky,

But don't look back, there's nothing there to see

Put a hand on your heart, for that is where I'll be.

Fourteen

Remember When I Told You

Remember when I told you that youth is wasted on the young?

These words I still hold true.

There's so much to experience and to enjoy,

And that's my gift to you.

Never let anyone make you feel,

That you're not good enough.

Ignore those whose aim is to put you down,

You're my daughter, made of stronger stuff!

Challenges you must face,

But you will overcome.

As the strength you have inside you

Creates the person you'll become.

Remember when I told you that time is the greatest prize?

Spend it wisely, make every moment count.

Your life will never be defined,

By a cautiously saved amount.

Promise me you'll live listening to your heart,

Wear it on your sleeve.

Think of all we've spoken about,

It'll help you while you grieve.

FIFTEEN

— ◦ —

RAINDROPS

Look for me in raindrops as they fall to the ground,

Hear me in the wind as your name I sound.

My voice will always echo the love I felt for you,

Look for me in the morning, fresh in springtime's dew.

Feel me take your hand when troubles make you sad,

Touch me in your heartbeat, feel the love we had.

My arms will be around you, holding you so close,

Feel me in your soul, the one I love the most.

Sixteen
—·—

Sunrise

Everyday the sun will rise, that doesn't mean it shines,

Sometimes it hides away, hoping for better times.

But look how stunning the light is, welcoming a new day,

Silence is so powerful when you don't know what to say.

Memories shine brightly, reflecting in that light,

Hold on to those moments for comfort through the night.

For once the sun has set, the mind wanders again in sleep,

To all those precious memories, they are yours to keep.

SEVENTEEN

— · —

THE NOTES THAT LIFE PLAYS

A walk on the beach feeling the sand in your toes,

Remembering how the beat of our song goes.

How music can trigger an instant precious thought,

The love for those notes, simply cannot be taught.

Your own melody created in your heart,

Captures what you've searched for, from the very start.

The notes that life plays begin the day we're born,

Bringing here together, all of those who mourn

This maestro of life who now returns to earth,

A beautiful soul who gives the tune its worth.

Both the sad notes and the happy songs,

Sing that soul back, to exactly where it belongs.

Eighteen

The Poppy

A poppy falls and lands upon the grave,
Of the fallen hero, so young and so brave.
The poppy floats in the autumn breeze.
As we remember battles on both land and seas.

You stood as brothers-in-arms ready to defend,
The territory you love, the life of your friend.
As the sun sets and there's no more letters to write,
No words express the horrors of this fight.

Forced silence hides fear in those words of truth,
Of those poor young men, scarred in the prime of youth.
The brave and the scorned standing side by side,
United in honour with your Country's pride.

Nineteen

We Are Not Separated

We are not separated by death,
Only by the clockface on display.
Sadly your time was reached,
As mine will be one day.

I know the pain you felt,
Became too much to bear.
You left me all those memories,
I know you truly care.

I promise I will remember,
All the kind words you have said,
As I walk my path alone,
Embracing where I tread.

The time we had together
Will always make me smile.
I held you for many years,
Just stay with me a while.

Let me feel your arms around me,

Shielding me from this grief.

Send me a loving sign,

To offer some relief.

For I shall look for you always,

On earth and in the sky,

And when I feel you close to me,

My eyes will eventually dry.

The tears have been free falling,

This pain so uninvited,

But in my dreams you came to me,

My heart feels us reunited.

Twenty

There's a Light Shining

There's a light shining through the window, is it too dim to see?

I long to create memories again, just you and me.

I don't want to let sadness overshadow good times that we shared.

Hoping that you know, just how much I cared.

Moments not taken for granted; how could we have known,

That I'd be taken suddenly, before the children grown?

To those who stand and mourn me, smile when you hear my name,

Just as when I feel your thoughts of love, I shall do the same.

Twenty-One

Precious Memories

A memory may be private, never needing to be shared,
A moment back in time, showing how you cared.
Being close to a person, brings many thoughts to mind,
How they were so loving, how they were so kind.

A person leads their life, making choices along the way,
And when the time comes, that they could no longer stay,
The essence of their soul, remains with those they love,
So when you feel them close to you, smile and look above.

A memory appears, when thoughts are wandering free,
Allowing them this freedom often is the key.
Embrace the love they have for you, that will never leave,
As your own heart responds allowing you to grieve.

Now listen to your precious memories, cherished as they are,
Look up towards the night sky and choose the brightest star.
Remember that for grief to exist, love has played a big part,
Take all those precious memories and keep them in your heart.

TWENTY-TWO

No Words

No words can express what I feel inside,

I wish I could have seen,

How to protect you from wanting to hide.

How different things may have been.

I understand that your pain was strong,

A force that took control.

What you did wasn't wrong,

It was how you could free your soul.

When thoughts of you come to mind,

I'll always make the space,

To remember you as loving and kind,

Just too troubled for this place.

My love for you will never die,

And it shall never fade.

I know how hard you had to try,

With no way you could have stayed.

No words to comfort those,

Who search within for peace.

I respect with unconditional love,

Your choice of final release.

Twenty-Three

I Could Never Leave

The value of life can simply be measured,

By those moments that will always be treasured.

True sentiment is bound to the heart,

And our souls will never be apart.

You see, I'll never leave you, our love is so strong,

Something we've both known for oh so very long.

Please don't cry, let me dry your eyes,

Instead, look for me in a different guise.

You have to live life and not create a shrine,

Remember when I promised that I'd leave a sign?

Here it is my darling, every time you breathe

For you are the one love who I could *never* leave.

Twenty-Four

Here I Stand

Here I stand

Photo in hand

Thinking of times gone by.

My eyes close

My heart knows

It was your time to fly.

Memories remain,

Love is the same.

I knew you couldn't stay.

My heart sings

About all the things

Enjoyed before you were taken away.

I understand

This wasn't planned,

And I mustn't remain in the dark.

I remember yet,

When we first met

Just how captivating was our spark.

You made me

So happy

And that I'll always hold dear.

I realise

That closing my eyes

Allows me to feel you right here.

I always will

Love you until

The very end of time.

Memories stay

In my heart every day

And forever you'll be mine.

TWENTY-FIVE

CAST MY LINE

Lead me to the waters' edge and let me cast my line.

This is for me, the perfect place to spend my time.

There is peace to be found fishing on the high seas,

Reeling in the catch with well-crafted expertise.

To some it's only fishing, to me it's part of life,

Luckily I have the support of my adoring wife.

Fishing is a way for the mind to explore,

The wonders of the water, the secrets of the shore.

Angling for the prize, bait prepared with real care,

Sit back with patience in the comfy fishing chair.

A bite may appear, the line starts to move,

This is pure enjoyment, there's nothing to prove.

Understanding the terrain, precision at its best,

Only when the nets are full will I have a rest.

A satisfying day, a catch fit for a King,

Fishing has always made my heart sing.

The stillness of the open water, the sun warming skin,

Each tug on the rod for me is a win.

As I now lay my rod to rest, for the final time,

I'll treasure those memories, of how I cast my line.

Twenty-Six

Pour the Tea

I'll join you for tea in a while,

Pour or keep it in the pot.

Use the cosy if you must,

Just make sure it stays hot.

You remember how I like it?

Put the milk in first.

There's nothing better than a cup of tea,

To quench an old lady's thirst.

Did you bring the biscuits,

The ones from my tin?

You know the ones I like

Those with the chocolate in.

I long to reach out and tell you,

That I am now pain free.

But let's just sit and be together,

And enjoy our cup of tea.

TWENTY-SEVEN

THE SOUND OF FOOTBALL

Can you hear the crowd

Warming up with their song?

The sound of football,

You've loved for so long.

The colours you support,

Earned a place in your heart,

Which beats so much faster,

Just before the start.

Stranger standing on the terrace,

With this magic that you share.

The sound of football joins you,

Like the colours that you wear.

The bond here is solid,

Before the first whistle blows,

Proud of the shirt you wear,

Proud of the team you chose.

In those first few moments,

The energy lights up faces,

As each and every fan there,

Succumbs and embraces

The sound of football,

That sings to your soul,

Craving that special moment,

Savouring every goal!

Twenty-Eight

The Flowers in Your Garden

The flowers are still growing,

You looked after them well.

Beautiful colours,

And a sweetness of smell.

A walk in the garden,

To see a reflection of you.

So vibrant the flowers dance,

And each year they'll renew.

I used to watch from the window,

As you tended the flowers.

Now I sit amongst them,

Reflecting here for hours.

Here in your space,

The sun often beams.

I take these precious moments,

For comfort in my dreams.

Twenty-Nine

Oh Daughter of Mine

A reflective walk along the coast
Understanding what I value most.
As I child I had freedom to go off and discover,
The world in my own steps but guided by my mother.

She taught me, encouraged me, to find a path of my own,
Knowing I always had the security of home.
So many places I go where I remember her clearly,
And feel that warmth of how she loved me so dearly.

Life must go on, I'm ready to face what lies ahead,
As I remember those poignant words she once said.
'When life throws a challenge, don't bury your head and hide,
Walk your path with purpose, obstructions brush aside.

And if conflict arises, stand up and fight,
No one can ever put out a fire that's alight.
Whatever you believe in will make your own life shine,
But always strive for happiness, oh daughter of mine!'

Thirty

A Man Can

A man can leave an impression, one that lasts forever,

Wonderful memories of those wonderful times together.

These can never be taken, they are yours to keep,

In every waking moment and when you fall asleep.

A man can leave a lesson, written in the sand,

In moments of sadness, feel him take your hand.

You walked with him in life, you will in memory too,

Knowing that he loved and cared deeply for you.

A man can make you smile, even from the sky,

Embracing you in your sadness, willing you not to cry.

His strength is always with you, never fading pride,

Whenever you feel lonely, he'll be there by your side.

Here lies such a man, wore his heart upon his sleeve,

And although the pain is real, the time is now to grieve.

And on those days, when nothing makes sense,

Remember grief and love are entwined, powerful and intense.

Just as he was in life, so shall he now remain,

A man who fills your thoughts time and time again.

Leave here today, with memories in your heart,

Think of him often and you'll never be apart.

Thirty-One

Do Not Be Afraid

Do not be afraid to still speak my name,

The memories we share shall not be in vain.

Imagine I'm here beside you, holding you tight,

As you struggle to sleep through the night.

The pain I had has left me, now I can breathe,

The only thing that hurt was that I had to leave.

Words often cannot express what you truly mean,

I promise I will comfort you in every lucid dream.

Do not be afraid to remember the happy times we shared,

Imagine me close to you when you're feeling scared.

Black was never my colour, nor shall it be in death,

Whisper my name and hold it on your breath.

You don't need a place in which to speak to me,

I'll always be close now my soul has been set free.

The strength you have inside you is powerful and strong,

There's a place in your heart where I will forever belong.

Thirty-Two

Celebrate My Life

I knew I was dying and soon I'd have to leave,

But I'd rather see you smiling than cry as you grieve.

We spoke about my funeral, that black must not be worn,

I'd like a celebration, like on the day I was born.

I've lived my life well, achieved much that I desired,

Then my body told me it was starting to get tired.

You all rallied round me, I can't thank you enough,

I know to see me weaken, that must have been tough.

I am proud of you all, with my children I am blessed,

So here's my final legacy, to you all I bequest,

The freedom to explore, continue adventures of your own,

Nurture your own children until the time is known.

They too, will want to fly the nest. Your blessing must be given,

Their characters remind me of you, so energetically driven.

Please celebrate my life, and try not to be sad,

Remember all the good times, and for those be glad.

I love you darling children. You made my life complete.

I'll always be with you. We share one true heartbeat.

For a mother never dies, she just steps aside,

Watching her family grow with love and enormous pride.

Thirty-Three

Always Too Young

I never expected

To be subjected

To a life where my parents are gone.

It all feels

So unreal

I don't know how to go on.

Anniversaries arrive,

I contrive

To step out from the dark.

Strongly, I grieve,

Without reprieve

My life has lost its spark.

Nothing prepares

Nor compares

To the times we spent together.

You gave so much,

A parental touch

Symbolised now by a falling white feather.

My heart broken

No last words spoken,

I often cry myself to sleep.

Yet thankful I am

That I still can,

Have all those memories to keep.

Goodnight to you,

Life begins anew

I'm grateful for all the lessons shared.

I know inside,

You were filled with pride

And from the bottom of your hearts, you cared.

Thirty-Four

Furry Friend

Their love is unconditional,

You see it in their eyes.

Every time they see you,

It's a wonderful surprise.

Nothing can replace,

The bond between you two.

You are their world

And they, the same to you.

When the day arrives,

That their heart no longer beats.

A sadness consumes you,

Not fixed with tasty treats.

Remember all the years,

Spent with your furry friend.

They loved you unconditionally

Right through until the end.

Thirty-Five

Dance With Me

He leads her to the dance floor,

As the music starts to play.

Her dress sways with the rhythm,

There's none so in time as they.

It's as though two souls are dancing,

Aligning now as one.

Their eyes locked in a loving gaze,

This is their memory song.

Thirty-Six

Don't Let Me Be

Don't let me be the one to stand in your way,

I would hate for you to regret it someday.

I've seen the look that's in your eyes,

Your true feelings are no surprise.

One thing I've learnt from a wonderful Mum,

Is that you can't please all, maybe only some

But there's only ONE person you need to impress

Only one person to whom you must confess.

The answers will always hide in your eyes,

The honesty that the truth can't disguise.

Life is too short to play by the rules,

Mix with smart people, ditch the fools.

Lead with your heart, backed up by your head

Don't stand still, leap forward instead.

Have faith in the power that's deep inside

Not dampened by the tears that have now dried.

There's a strength within you that will conquer fear

Or give you a well-needed kick up the rear.

So don't let me be the one to stand in your way,

I would hate for you to regret it someday.

THIRTY-SEVEN

— • —

YOU KNOW TOO MUCH MY FRIEND

How many nights have we laughed over nothing in particular?

Or wiped away tears of a broken heart?

To explain the value of a friend like you, where could I possibly start?

From the moment we declared ourselves as besties,

We set a code in stone. No matter what time of day or night,

I've never felt alone.

Over the years you've been there unconditionally,

Our bond is our true strength. For you I would do anything,

Go to any length.

I realised quite quickly we could never **not** be friends,

And upon this bold statement,

My integrity depends!

So, let's make an eternal promise. One we shall uphold,

That should something happen to one of us,

NONE of this be told!

Thirty-Eight

Our First Kiss

No one was looking,
You leaned in with grace,
And plonked a whopping smacker
In the middle of my face.

Next time it went smoother,
You aimed for my lips.
I felt your exploring hand,
Rest upon my hips.

These kisses they got better,
We practiced when we could.
Happy with each other
Life with you was good.

When you asked to marry
I couldn't catch my breath,
Our vows were very sacred,
To be parted only by death.

The dress I wore that day
Is imprinted in my mind.
So beautiful yet simple,
A perfect one-of-a-kind.

We worked hard to build,
A life filled with bliss,
And if things got tough,
I'd think of our first kiss.

From a small beginning,
We sought hard to find
And were extremely lucky
Our lives became entwined.

Thirty-Nine

The Cantankerous Old Git

The cantankerous old git

Was happy to sit

And moan about people's behaviour.

He liked to drink

And used to think

He was his local pub's saviour.

But deep down inside

He'd try to hide

The softer side he possessed.

No one must know

Just how far he'd go

To keep his kindness repressed.

If you were to ask

Him to do a task

He'd bark back at you a clear NO!

But if you sat

There was a chance that

He'd explain why blow by blow.

Cantankerous he was
Brought on because
His father was just the same.
Two peas in a pod
The little sod
Treated being stroppy as a game.

But once in while
He'd crack a smile,
And perhaps you'd join in too.
For in life he became
The one to blame
For having given life to you!

Dear old dad
You said don't be sad
With honesty I'll remember you here.
You taught me much
Life lessons and such,
The funny ones I'll always hold dear

But now we must
In our emotions trust
And say get through this one final bit.
So we raise a glass

To the pain in the arse

But who was OUR cantankerous old git!

Forty

--- ◆ ---

The Truth

Let's all gather round the table,

There's something I want to share.

There's room for us all,

Just pull up a chair.

So many times we've sat here,

And talked about our day.

But how different the conversation would be,

If we spoke the truth in all we say.

Would you tell your grandma,

She had whiskers on her chin,

Or would you simply be a darling

And pour her another gin?

What about the elder sibling,

With whom you've always fought.

Would you poke them in the eye,

Negating the manners I taught?

Your spouse sits beside you,

Would you speak the truth,

Of how you were a nightmare,

When dating in your youth?

Sometimes the truth is better,

Hidden from the now.

Not all words must be spoken,

And for the silence please allow.

Look around this table,

Each person is so unique.

It's you, the family rebel,

The one they call black sheep.

One gift you always have,

Is to keep conversations real.

They won't remember what you said,

Just how you made them feel.

Forty-One

Passing By

She's standing there, lonely in the crowd,

Hands covering her face, the noise too loud.

She longs to reach out

Show him she's here

She longs to shout

But is drowning in tears.

He walks past, doesn't recognise her face,

Oblivious to both this time and place.

She tries to call

Get him to see

She tries not to fall

Get him not to flee.

To much time has passed, the water is too deep,

The memories have faded, shadows now keep

A Love unable to survive the polluted mind

Of a lover, who was once so gentle and kind

He's standing here, looking into space,

Desperately trying to search for her face.

He has no voice

To try and speak

He has no choice

But to turn his cheek.

Too much time has passed, words cannot be unsaid,

There's no hope of sunshine on their path ahead.

Their ships have passed, no sails have been lowered,

No one climbed the mast, too proud, both cowered.

Set the compass and leave this place,

The only memory, the love on her face.

Set the compass and sail with your dreams,

Scatter your broken heart, amongst sun beams.

Forty-Two

More Than An Emotion

Grief is more than an emotion,

It's a process we go through.

There's no rule book to follow.

It becomes a part of you.

Each time you feel it rising,

Knowing pain's about to hit.

Find a comfy place,

And rest there for a bit.

The waves may come crashing.

You think you've lost control.

As your heart is aching,

For the one whose breath grief stole.

Although we try with words,

None are right to say.

We have to ride this feeling out,

When grief comes into play.

Take all the time you need.

Grief isn't to be ignored.

A complex ride of emotions,

Each one needs to be explored.

ACKNOWLEDGEMENTS

Thank you, Sue Steel, for the wonderful cover design. It's wonderful to see you rediscovering your artistic talents.

To Marge, Tone, and Gilly, thank you for checking my words make sense!

Rebecca Raisin for those 4am conversations and writing bursts that finally gave me the push I needed to finish this book and start the next one. Our 'let's do it' mantra lives on.

Some people come into your life for a reason and I am so glad Alex, (Rosie) owner of Whitmey Funeral Directors in Sittingbourne, came into mine. He gave me the opportunity to discover whether I could work within the funeral industry. That leap of faith, on both parts, began one of the most wonderful relationships and I am proud to be part of the Whitmey family.

Finally, thank you to all the families I have had the honour of meeting as a Funeral Celebrant. Thank you for inspiring me with stories of times gone by and for trusting me to take care of your loved ones. You have inspired many of these poems.

ABOUT THE AUTHOR

Hilary Steel lives in Kent and is always working on a writing project of some sort when not working as a Funeral Celebrant. Personal experience inspires much of her writing; sometimes it's humorous and sometimes it captures deeper sentiments. Either way, she always writes from the heart.

'Moments in Time'–'Uplifting Poems for Grieving Hearts' is a selection of poems Hilary wrote inspired by the complexities of emotions grief can cause.

When not with pen in hand, you will probably find her in the kitchen playing with ingredients, hoping to create a culinary masterpiece.

Hilary would love to connect with you so please visit Instagram or Twitter @hilaryjsteel

www.hilarysteel.com

Printed in Great Britain
by Amazon

42659945R00046